Presented to

_____

By

_____

On the Occasion of

_____

Date

_____

$\mathcal{T}$o my daughter, Deborah Dawn Martin Jewell,
who as a child had to find her way along sorrow's path.

I admire you for your strong faith in God.
You did come forth as gold.

What comfort and joy you always are to me
as you continue your walk with our God
every day of your life.

©MCMXCVIII by Barbour Publishing, Inc.

ISBN 1-57748-203-4

Published by Barbour Publishing, Inc.
P.O. Box 719
Uhrichsville, Ohio 44683
http://www.barbourbooks.com

Member of the
Evangelical Christian
Publishers Association

Printed in the United States of America.

Sorrowing in HOPE

A Path of Healing
for the Bereaved

Elva Minette Martin

BARBOUR
PUBLISHING, INC.
Uhrichsville, Ohio

Dear Friend,

I cannot tell what you're feeling just now. Or maybe you don't feel anything. You are simply numbed by your loss and would just as soon let life go on without you.

I've walked down the path of loss. I've struggled through days and nights of endless hours. It was as if I were watching a drama going on all around me. I hated this story with all my passion, and yet I couldn't make it stop.

God carried me in His arms all the way through. He was and is my stability, my strength, and my song. Oh yes, He even restored a song of praise in my soul.

I'd like to walk with you through these most difficult days. Perhaps if we share the way, the journey will be a little easier.

Yours in the fellowship of suffering,
Elva

SORROW IN HOPE

Sorrow not. . .as others which have no hope.
1 Thessalonians 4:13

Sorrow not? I've had to release the dearest to me on earth. My dear one is not to be found. I am alone, confused, sad, fearful. And God says sorrow not?

Sorrow not? But Jesus wept at the grave of Lazarus. Later, sitting on a hill overlooking Jerusalem, He mourned those who refused to accept Him.

Sorrow, heartache, and tears are all natural responses to the painfulness of separation. God does not ask that I do not sorrow. He knows the impossibility of that right now. God's Word to me is *to* SORROW, but not as if I had no hope. For I know that my dear one and I will be together forever!

I cannot help the anguished pangs of a heavy heart. Such pain may be present for a season, maybe for a long time. But I should know that this is normal, natural, reasonable. Loss hurts.

I can walk through this valley of sadness and emerge victoriously. Final victories often are reached after lengthy battles. So I will grieve as is needful today, hoping that tomorrow will be a little easier.

THROUGH WITH MY GOD

I have walked through the Red Sea of dread and of fear,
    The foreboding of sorrow and loss;
But my God went before me and opened the sea,
    'Neath my feet I felt strength from the cross.

Tho' my heart was abreaking, my eyes dimmed by tears,
    My soul crying out for relief,
Yet my Lord held the waters on right hand and left;
    I was not overcome by my grief!

So I, clinging to His Word, along sorrow's path
    Where He led me, in confidence trod;
And He held back the waters that could have overwhelmed;
    I WENT ALL THE WAY THROUGH WITH MY GOD!

$\mathcal{B}$ut the children of Israel
walked upon dry land in the
midst of the sea;
and the waters were a wall unto them
on their right hand, and on their left.
Thus the LORD saved Israel that day...
And Israel saw that great work
which the LORD did. . .
and believed the LORD.

Exodus 14:29–31

I'M GETTING ALONG
VERY WELL?

Does it seem that I'm getting along well? Do I look like I'm making it? The many masks I wear all disguise my true heart. No one sees the inner desolation or feels the fears, those swordlike piercings through my heart.

Somehow life must continue. I only know how my heart fairly cries out for my dear one, for relief from the crushing pain of my loss.

> How long wilt Thou forget me, LORD? for ever?
> How long wilt thou hide thy face from me? . . .
> Consider and hear me, O LORD my God:
> lighten mine eyes, lest I sleep the sleep of death.
> *Psalm 13:1, 3*

I've struggled to stay on top—but I can't do it! Maybe I would rather just sleep that sleep. It would seem so much easier than continuing on in this life. Oh Lord, don't leave me here. I want to be in heaven with my dear one.

> In the LORD put I my trust:
> how say ye to my soul,
> Flee as a bird to your mountain?
> *Psalm 11:1*

I want to flee all of this life, Father. But You say that I should put my trust in Your mercy. I guess that means to continue here in Your arms until all the calamities of this life are concluded. You will carry me through, won't You, Father?

Yes, I know that You will carry me all the way through!

LEAN HARD

Today nothing hurts. I simply don't feel. I am numbed by my grief.

Sadness has closed me in until nothing matters. Nothing can be changed. Nothing can be helped. There are no reverses in this thing called death. Since nothing can be done, I need do nothing. I wonder whether this nightmare will go away if I just wait long enough.

There is no reason to get out of bed this morning. There is no reason for today to be, for me to exist today. . .no reason except that God has left me here for SOMETHING. But I surely don't know what it is.

Oh, God, help me look up. Help me to see You and to feel Your strength in my inner depths. My physical body needs strength too, Lord. I'm so weak. Help me! Carry me through this world of sorrow and dying.

> Fear thou not; for I am with thee: be not dismayed;
>> for I am thy God: I will strengthen thee;
>> yea, I will help thee; yea, I will uphold thee. . . .
> I. . .will hold thy right hand. . .Fear not; I will help thee.
>> *Isaiah 41:10, 13*

The LORD our Redeemer gave these promises. The LORD our Redeemer cannot fail.

I will lean hard upon Him.

WHAT IF. . . ?

What if we hadn't lived here? What if we had gone to a doctor sooner? What if we had not left home that day? What if. . .?

There are so many things that could have been different. If my dear one had not been at that place then. . .if 1 had done something more to help. . .if we hadn't waited so long. . .if we had waited longer. . . .

As I try to figure out what could have prevented the death of my dear one, I realize that human reasoning is incapable of changing a human destiny.

I may as well not ponder the "what ifs." It is too late to change anything.

Nursing guilt feelings will not help me now.

Worry will not help me now.

And my dear one does not need any help now.

I guess the most sensible, reasonable step I can take is to consent to accept this separation and sorrow as God's will for me.

I can accept today as God's gift to me.

I can trust Him to hold me up and to lead me through this moment.

What if I can't make it?

I CAN!

I can do all things through Christ
who strengthens me.
Philippians 4:13 NKJV

*O*f His perfect love
He gives to me unmeasured,
Of His grace enough
and strength to meet my day,
Secrets of His own dear heart
He lays before me,
Then enables me
to follow in His way.

I WILL BE ALL RIGHT

"Everything will be all right." That's what concerned friends say. And they don't always say it glibly either. Often they simply do not know what words of comfort to offer and they sincerely wish they could make everything right for me.

At least they understand that things are NOT right! They are not the same, not what I am used to. My home is empty and that leaves my heart feeling the same. My arms ache to embrace my dear one. But that will never be again on earth.

On earth! I did say that, didn't I? Somehow that suggests a limit to this hopelessness of "never again."

God has put a limit on never. *Never,* as I have used it here, means "not for the remainder of this temporary life." But forever awaits!

And forever and forever everything will be all right!

Until forever comes, I will be all right.

For He careth for me.

Casting all your care upon him; for he careth for you.
1 Peter 5:7

HOME

No certain dwelling place here on this earth—
    But I'm on my way HOME.
I am a stranger, an alien by birth—
    But I'm on my way HOME.
Wearying miles and uphill I must tread,
Walking by faith in the path Jesus said,
Looking to Him as my strength and my stay,
Knowing one time I'll reach the end of my day;
In the embrace of my Savior so dear,
Welcoming words will descend on my ear:
    My Child, you are at HOME!

LOST

Father, mother, sister, brother, husband, wife, child, or dearest friend . . .no matter who, well-meaning friends will say, "I'm so sorry you've lost your dear one."

Lost?

Well, yes, I have lost companionship here on earth.

I have lost their physical presence; my dear one cannot be seen or touched.

Lost is the comfortable conversation we shared.

These "things" that I've lost are the joys I once had because of my dear one. But these "things," the comfortable and glad times of life, are not my dear one. After having lost his dear wife of thirty-three years, Vance Havner, the great gospel preacher and evangelist said, "You can't say that something is lost when you know where it is."

I know exactly where my dear one is—in God's immediate presence, living, safe, happy now and for all eternity. Not lost! No, not by any means! Not lost to God or to me! My dear one has only gone on ahead. Someday, when I arrive, we'll be able to live together there in God's presence—forever!

Together forever—
what joy it will be!
Together with Jesus
for eternity!
Together with loved ones,
never to part,
Together within
the love of God's heart!

Whether we wake or sleep,
we should live together with Him.
1 Thessalonians 5:10

AT HOME

I am a stranger here on earth. I never realized that fact more than I do now. Here I am, left alone, feeling my dear one's absence keenly.

Lord, I know my dear one trusted You as Savior and so now is in Your immediate presence. But what is it like to be there?

I thank You, Lord, for stooping to my weakness and showing me these truths from Your Word. My dear one is...

LIVING. . . . . 1 Thessalonians 5:10;
John 11:26
KNOWING . . . . 1 Corinthians 13:12
ENJOYING. Philippians 1:23
HAPPY AND RESTING . . . . Revelation 14:13
COMFORTED .Luke 16:25
SUBMISSIVE. Romans 14:9
EMBODIED . . . . 2 Corinthians 5:1–4
CLOTHED. Revelation 19:8
SERVING. Revelation 22:3,4
NOT LIMITED (needs no sleep). . . . . Revelation 22:5

SATISFIED . . . . .Revelation 7:16,17
REWARDED. . . . . 1 Corinthians 3:14; 4:5

I believe God wants me to stop searching and yield to Him my dear one's situation. Whatever God does is right and perfect.

Thank You, Lord, for these precious truths You have shown me, for the comfort they are.

Thank You for loving me so much that You will share Your secrets with me. Full understanding—well worth waiting for—will be mine in heaven.

Thank You, Lord, that I am the stranger here on earth. In heaven my dear one is right at home!

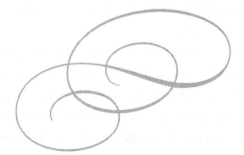

GAZING INTO GLORY

The sun was setting as I made my way to my favorite secluded spot along the riverbank. Trees lining the opposite bank were dressed in a rainbow of fall colors, a natural wonder mirrored in the lightly rippling waters.

I reached my log and sat to enjoy the splendor and peacefulness of God's creation. Smiling down from a very blue sky was a full moon. Glorious!

How I longed to see right through that blue, right past that moon and into God's heaven! My heart is already there. Certainly the glory is far, far beyond anything we could ever imagine. *What is it like to be there?* I wondered for the millionth time. Tears fell down my cheeks but I wasn't embarrassed because I was alone with my God. I talked to Him; I even sang.

I remained seated as darkness slowly overtook the evening sky. I waited to see when the first star would become visible.

The old hymn of Annie Ross Cousin, "The Sands of Time are Sinking," reminds me that in heaven one's focus will not be on glory or crowns but on the face of our Beloved. My dear one is looking on

Jesus, the bright and morning Star!

I know now that I would not wish my dear one to return to me in this land of sorrow. Oh, no! I'll try to be patient as I wait God's time for our reunion. I know my dear one has never been safer or happier!

And one day I'll be in glory, too.

> For now we see through a glass darkly;
> but then face to face.
> *1 Corinthians 13:12*

WHAT WILL IT BE?

What will it be
> to see His face,
> to hold His nail-pierced hand,
> to worship at His blessed feet
> and dwell in heaven's land?

What will it be
> to part no more,
> to know no sin or woe,
> to never again feel pain or tears
> in that land to which I go?

What will it be?
> I cannot tell,
> nor can my fancy free,
> envision even a part of all
> my Beloved has prepared for me!

SORTING

My dear one really is gone from this earthly life—for always. My dear one's earthly goods will not be needed again. I must sort through them and decide what to do with clothing, papers, and jewelry.

But how can I bring myself to face this task, to pack, give away, throw away? I feel the desire to clutch. I know things ought not to be so important. But somehow they are part of what I've lost and I don't want to lose anymore. I want to let the things sit as they are. But my sister says she will help me and it is best to do it soon.

Oh, my Heavenly Father, help me! I am in such dazed state of mind that You, my God, will have to take over and show me the right decisions.

Yes, the tears flow. Yes, the memories linger and bring longings. Yes, it will hurt to have all these things gone, but I need to separate from the earthly part of my dear one. Maybe I'll be able to think more of what it must be like up there.

Maybe with the putting away of things, God will give grace to begin to forget what cannot be restored on earth, and to look forward.

$\mathcal{T}$hou art my refuge and my portion
in the land of the living. . .
Bring my soul out of prison,
that I may praise thy name. . .
for thou shalt deal bountifully with me.

Psalm 142:5, 7

WHAT TIME IS IT?

The days and nights have come and gone. How many? I really don't know. It seems that time has simply dropped off my calendar and I can't get back in place.

I must need to do so many things. Yet I wonder what it is that I ought to do next. Does it matter whether I do it or not? The hours follow one upon another. What is there to show for my living?

Impossible—everything! Except with God.

I don't know that I've ever before lived so completely a moment at a time.

My comfort is my Father God. I find that I may ask His direction, for help and for the desire to keep on living. The knowledge that His hands are capable of enabling me is truly strengthening. He is in control of my being—physical and spiritual, emotional and intellectual.

What time is it? I do not know and I'm not real concerned about the calendar or the clock on the wall. But I am sure that constantly it is time for me to seek the Lord and His strength.

Seek the LORD, and His strength: seek His face evermore.
Psalm 105:4

PAINFUL FIRSTS

I went to church today. God is gracious to uphold me, yet these "firsts" are certainly painful. I kept looking to my right, hoping to find my dear one sitting next to me.

Family came to share a meal with me, but that one place at the table was so empty.

Evenings are the worst. We ought to be all at home together! The absent one leaves a prominent vacancy.

Jesus left home and Father and came to this troubled world. The scorn and rejection must have pained His heart. Those nails certainly caused physical anguish.

I am thankful that God told us of Jesus' grief when John the Baptist's life was taken. Jesus' disciples gave John a fitting burial. Then Jesus went away to a quiet place to rest a while with only His closest friends (Matthew 14).

Jesus wept with the bereaved sisters beside the grave of Lazarus. He took to His own heart their agony and misery (John 11).

Jesus "in the days of his flesh. . .offered up prayers and supplications with strong crying and tears unto him that was able to save him

. . .and was heard. . ." (Hebrews 5:7).

Jesus prayed with strong emotion when He was on the earth. And God heard Him. Yet He learned obedience to God "by the things which he suffered" (Hebrews 5:8).

God is perfecting my life, too. He is teaching me through grief and suffering to walk closer to Him. He is helping me to become like His own Son.

> Lord Jesus, live Your life in me,
>   In all of Your sufficiency;
> For body, soul, and mind, as well,
>   Thyself enough—oh in me dwell.
>
> Yea, Lord, O make Thyself at home,
>   Thy life in me, my heart Thy throne;
> Thyself, Thy fullness I receive;
>   Thy grace enables to believe.
>
> Praise God! Praise God! In Christ I rest,
>   Forever secure upon His breast;
> He's all I need for now and aye—
>   Himself throughout eternal day.

I'LL NEVER LOVE AGAIN

I think I'll say it and maybe the words will help me somehow to face it: "I never want to love anyone again because I'm so afraid."

Maybe then it won't hurt so much when family goes home, when friends are busy somewhere else, when someone else I know dies.

Maybe I can adopt a neutral, uncaring attitude, a take-it-or-leave-it relationship with family and friends. If I enjoy their love and kindness to me, then I know I will hurt too much when they have to go on with their own lives.

But I can't carry out this attitude completely. I find myself crying to God not to let this loved one die or that friend move away. My family and friends are being so supportive of me through these difficult days and I love them.

Father God, I know You will always be with me. How can I even want to love anyone other than You? Oh, Lord, You remind me that You give all things richly to enjoy—now! Could that include people? You loved Your only Son, but You were willing to be separated from Him. You let Him leave You. You let Him die. But You also knew the Resurrection was to follow. . . .

Hallelujah! I know that, too! Separations are only for time, and time will be finished soon. Then we will be together in Your love, Father. Forever!

GOD HAS PROVIDED FOR TODAY;
WILL HE NOT DO THE SAME FOR TOMORROW?

This is my commandment,
that ye love one another,
as I have loved you.
John 15:12

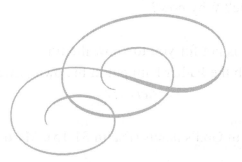

WHY?

Why? Why? I cannot explain why God would want to take my dear one. We were so happy. Oh, life wasn't perfect, but at least we were facing it together. Is this to punish me?

I wondered if it could possibly please God to cause me such grief. Then I remembered that it pleased Him to bruise His own Son, to put Him to grief (Isaiah 53:10). When Jesus died on my behalf, He died so that I—and all who believe in Him—might have eternal life with Him.

God loved me that much, enough to let His own heart be broken in order to save me!

He loves me that much today. He is not punishing me, but helping me learn to live like a child of the King of Kings.

Why? Why me? Why now?

> It is not for you to know the times. . .
> which the Father hath put in his own power.
> *Acts 1:7*

My times are in God's hands (Psalm 31:15). My dear one's times were also. I know God has His perfect plan for each life He has created.

Why? I cannot know all of God's answers. I would have to be God to know.

I think I do not need to know.

Why not let God be God?

Be still, and know that I am God.
Psalm 46:10

BOTTLES FOR MY TEARS

In Old Testament times, both in Egypt and Palestine, the tears of mourners were placed in clay bottles decorated with glass. Then the bottles were placed in the tomb.

Wouldn't that be wonderful to bury all tears, grief, and sorrow? But we know that tears are only an erupting of the wrenching grief that lingers long and deep inside of us. If tears were bottled and buried, that would neither assuage the grief nor heal the hurt.

The world says real men don't cry and big girls don't cry. But God does not look with contempt on my tears. They are not loathsome to Him. It is all right to weep.

In Psalm 56:8, David boldly tells God, "Put thou my tears into thy bottle." If God has a bottle for my tears, then He evidently notices my afflictions, He hears when I weep. Only He understands why He counts my tears as precious.

Psalm 22 refers to the affliction of Jesus Christ on the cross: "He hath not despised nor abhorred the affliction of the afflicted; neither hath he hid his face from him; but when he cried unto him, he heard" (verse 24). Jesus' sufferings were because of God's love, not because the Father despised Him.

I know I will be accepted at the Father's throne, tears and all. He tenderly loves me, hears the words I cannot say, and answers the desires of my heart.

One day He will wipe away all tears forever. Until then. . .

> Think not thou canst sigh a sigh,
>   And thy Maker is not by;
> Think not thou canst weep a tear,
>   And thy Maker is not near.
>
> Oh! He gives to us his joy,
>   That our grief he may destroy:
> Till our grief is fled and gone,
>   He doth sit by us and moan.

William Blake
from *Songs of Innocence* (1789)

THE DESIRES OF MY HEART

God knows the cherished desires of my heart. He knows that I want my dear one to be with me again. If only I could go back a few months in time, this separation would never have happened.

I simply cannot understand what God means when He says, "Delight thyself also in the LORD; and he shall give thee the desires of thine heart" (Psalm 37:4). I do love Him. These days especially I find all my hope, and any joy, to be in Him alone. But how does God plan to keep His promise to give me what I desire? I know my dear one will not come back to me.

A friend said there is no time limit on God's promises. When Jesus comes, I know my dear one and I will again be together—forever!

As I thought this through, I did have to admit to God that my deepest desire, the one even greater than wanting my dear one, is that God will be glorified. Maybe if people see that I can go on and live my life by God's grace, they will praise and honor Him.

Amy Carmichael, missionary to India for most of her life, wrote that neither in forgetting, nor endeavor, nor aloofness is peace—only in acceptance of sorrow. God, by Your grace, help me to trust Your choice for me.

God has promised that His grace will be sufficient. When He comes, every desire of my heart—and far more—will be fulfilled eternally. Even so, come, Lord Jesus.

Thou wilt keep him in perfect peace,
whose mind is stayed on thee:
because he trusteth in thee.
Isaiah 26:3

WHERE AM I WITH YOU, LORD?
WHAT DO YOU EXPECT OF ME?

Lord, am I walking with You? It seems I can't corral my thoughts to pray. Yet You always help me when I do call upon You. I think You must be answering my heart cries, too, when I don't even realize I'm praying.

I would like to spend time with You, to read Your Word at length. You never ask more than You supply. You understand when body and mind are totally exhausted.

My spirit is full of heaviness, my heart grieves.

Lord, where am I with You? Am I in Your will right now? What do You expect of me?

I know You want me to continue to live and bring glory to You.

Lord, thank You that one day I will realize a spirit of praise replacing the heaviness and grief.

Here I am, Lord, with You. We walk together and You hold my hand and lead me. You give me peace in our fellowship.

Thank You for staying when I have not been sensible or responsive.

Thank You for not leaving me alone.

Thank You that right now I feel safe and peaceful before You. Oh, how good it is to forget the whole world and just talk with You.

I guess what You expect is that I trust You right now.

Oh, I do, I do.

I love You, Lord.

It is God that girdeth me with strength,
and maketh my way perfect.
Psalm 18:32

My soul,
wait thou only upon God;
for my expectation is from him.
Psalm 62:5

I HAVE HELP

I almost turned to say, "I can't do this; I need your help." But immediately the realization returned that my dear one was not there, not anywhere available to me.

The sense of aloneness overwhelmed me. I have no help. I must figure it out alone. I must be responsible for all the details and final decisions.

> When I can do NOTHING
> about SOMETHING
> Then I can leave EVERYTHING
> in the hands of Him
> Who can do ALL THINGS!

I watched a small boy peddling his bike, balancing on the seat, steering with one hand, and clutching his books with the other hand. If only he had a basket, he could have given his whole attention to driving that bike.

Sometimes I go through my day just like the boy went down the road. I am carrying my sorrow, fears, worries. The boy had no choice. I do.

I may worry and be afraid if I want to, but I do have a place to lay my burdens. I have my God and He will carry the entire load. He even carried me through this little problem that loomed like a colossus in my mind.

Come to think about it, God has been continually carrying me every hour of every day and night. What concern do I have that would be too heavy for the God of heaven and earth to manage?

A promise from God is a fact. So to hope in God is to CONFI-DENTLY EXPECT that He will do as He promises.

God will carry the weight of all my cares if I let Him.

God even carries me!

I have help!

So that we may boldly say,
The Lord is my helper,
and I will not fear. . . .
Hebrews 13:6

WE

Not I today will do the task,
    But WE, my God and I;
Step by step we'll work along—
    I so frail: He so strong.

Not I today can stand the strife,
    But WE, my Savior and I;
Throughout the battle He's my shield,
    To His protection I gladly yield.

Not I today or ever.
    This flesh is no profit whatever!
My All in All in me shall stand
    And I just clinging to His hand.

REFLECTING

These days have been hard. I've experienced confusion, despair and depression, loneliness, fear, weakness.

Yet as I reflect, I can see some of the ways my Lord has carried my burdens. He has pled my cause at the Father's throne. He has caused my enemies to fall and perish at His presence.

For my impossibilities He has offered His ability.

For my inquisitiveness He has given His answers. They were not always the answers I could hope for, but they were perfectly correct and suited to my needs.

For my insecurities He has given assurance of safekeeping.

When I have despaired, He has given hope.

In my weakness He has given physical, emotional, and spiritual strength.

In lonely times, He has provided companionship. He is the Friend of friends. He is closer than a brother.

If I became confused, God rebuked the author of confusion, the wicked one. He had to flee and I was able to think clearly.

When I have felt depressed, He has filled my heart with praise and thanksgiving to replace the spirit of heaviness.

No matter what my need, I can receive supply from Him—if I will. Receiving brings rejoicing in Him. God has not left me alone to face this crisis. He has been there maintaining my cause constantly. He is on my side!

Since God is changeless, I know He will continue with me and for me, tomorrow...and forever.

I will praise Thee, O LORD, with my whole heart;
I will shew forth all thy marvellous works.
I will be glad and rejoice in Thee. . . .
Psalm 9:1, 2

I FEEL LIKE A LITTLE CHILD

I prayed aloud today with my sister. Later she said to me, "Do you know that you sounded just like a little child when you prayed?"

I feel like a little child today, carried in Father's arms, constantly provided for. I can feel God's love so near. I see God's hand caring for my every need. My Daddy, Father! Bless God!

> I had fainted, unless I had believed
> to see the goodness of the LORD
> in the land of the living.
> *Psalm 27:13*

$\mathcal{D}$raw me close to Thyself, Dear Lord,
   Hold me in Thy arms;
Pillow my head on Thy loving breast—
   Secure there from all alarms.

Fold me tenderly to Thy heart,
   Never to let me go;
Shelter me safe in Thy Presence,
   Apart from this world of woe.

Keep me forever there, Dear Lord,
   Thyself of joys my choice;
Above the dearest and best of life,
   In Thee I will rejoice.

Lift up Thy countenance upon me,
   And make Thy face to shine;
Let me rest beneath Thy wings—
   Forever Thou art mine!

And I am Thine! What need I more?

BEHAVING

How does the Lord want my life to proceed now that my dear one is gone? People tell me I need to find something meaningful to do—take a trip, get a job, or whatever I would like to do.

That's the problem—I really don't *want* to do anything. My whole body reacts as if in shock with chills, clamminess, and nausea when I think seriously of getting out and doing something, *anything*. Sometimes I feel afraid that I would cry at an inappropriate time or place. I wonder what to say to those well-meaning folk I'll meet, and they'll wonder what to say to me, too.

I've begun to pray about this and God has given me a goal from Psalm 131. The goal is to behave, to conduct myself as a true child of God, trusting in His choices for me.

During weaning children may fuss and be demanding. But when they learn to enjoy solid food, they become contented because the new food tastes good and satisfies. And Mother will yet be there loving, guiding, and providing.

So as I look to the future, I want to behave as the weaned child.

I want to trust my Father's wise provision for my needs—even though it isn't exactly what I'm used to.

I want to let Him teach me how to grow more independent. I won't forget Him, but will reach out to experience a new life in the wisdom and strength He will share with me.

I want to look to Him for grace not to fuss or fret but to contentedly follow in His way.

> Surely I have behaved and quieted myself,
> as a child that is weaned
> of his mother.
> *Psalm 131:2*

WHAT WILL I DO NOW?

Will my life go back to the usual, just as it was before? No, I am aware that my existence can never be the same. So much has changed, so much cannot be restored.

So where do I begin to put my life back together? I don't even know where to start. I recently heard someone say, "I don't want to go through the rest of my life just breathing in and out!" Nor do I.

I must go to my Heavenly Father: He knew, before the world was made, this heartache I would experience. He knows the end when something is only beginning. He has prepared the pathway and will go before and lead me.

God is able to bring beauty out of ashes. That's what my life seems like right now—ashes, the leftover charred portion of what was.

> My soul clings to the dust;
> Revive me. . .teach me. . .
> Make me understand the way of your precepts. . .
> Strengthen me according to Your word.
> *Psalm 119:25–28, NKJV*

God has set my feet on a firm foundation—faith in my unfailing, changeless God. He has given me life; He will help me understand how to use it to glorify Him. I have perfect peace in waiting on His leading.

> My future, Lord, what will it be?
>   My heart is troubled sore.
> Child, nestle closer unto Me,
>   Believe and fret no more.
>
> I'll lead the way and choices make,
>   You'll never walk alone;
> For I your God and confidence,
>   Will bring you safely Home.
>
> Frustration on Him freely roll,
>   In quietness find rest;
> A child in Refuge safe, secure
>   Upon his Father's breast.

Guidance and enabling for today are mine for the taking.

WHEN?

When shines the sun and darkness flees,
    When gone the chilling piercing breeze,
When all the world would smile at me—
    Then I will live in victory.

When never an ugly word I hear,
    When heart never aches, nor eye sheds tear,
When loving friends are always near—
    Then I the voice of God will hear.

Oh, all this life I'd wait for "when,"
    I'd sigh, complain, and long for "then,"
Except that God has made me know
    His faithfulness—He loves me so!

He sends the dark, the painful night,
 With tears He blesses me aright;
To be alone—a gift of grace,
 That I might gaze on His dear face.

All present things are mine, I see,
 Working together His good in me.
Thus NOW is when my soul can claim
 Triumph and peace in Jesus' name!

GRACE TO DO

I think of a shepherd with the crook of his staff drawing the sheep back from a dangerous precipice.

My Good Shepherd has done that for me. I've felt unable to fight or war. He has drawn me to Himself, kept me from pitfalls, and given spiritual victories over the wicked one.

When I can't do any more than rest in His love, His love is strong, sufficient, and sure.

I may not be ready to go out into life's battles of intercessory prayer or Christian service. Yet God is getting through to me, telling me that I do have to think about the future. I must be nearing His time for me to step out in faith. I don't know just what He desires, maybe that I go back to those folk I ministered to before my dear one died. (Say, I said that "d" word without much hesitation! Yes, I have already made a lot of progress toward getting back to normal life, whatever that is for me now.)

I'm thankful that I don't have to beg God for guidance. He has promised to guide His own continually. My responsibility is to follow Him. He will open and close the doors ahead. I will know His will. I will have grace to accept it (that part is vital!), and do it.

Now the God of peace. . .
make you perfect in every good work to do his will,
working in you that which is well-pleasing in his sight,
through Jesus Christ;
to whom be glory for ever and ever.
Amen.
Hebrews 13:20, 21

*H*e giveth more grace
and more and more
And always sufficient
Hc has in store;
The only price
that I must heed
Is that I bring
unto Him my need.

HOW LONG DOES IT TAKE TO HEAL?

We've often heard that time will heal. Time itself does not heal, or hinder. In their book *Comforting the Bereaved* (Moody Press, 1985), Warren and David Wiersbe have written that time is neutral. It is what we do with time that makes the difference.

But how much time does it take for a broken heart to heal? Each individual is unique. No one can say that a heart will heal in a certain number of weeks or months or years. To heal is a many-faceted process, as varied as people are diverse.

I am grateful for the patience of loved ones and close friends. They hurt with me and pray for me and encourage my restoration. Yet they do not berate me as I weep or struggle with inward pain. They also rejoice with me in each victory, no matter how small.

> My times are in thy hand. . .
> Let me not be ashamed, O LORD;
> for I have called upon thee. . . .
> *Psalm 31:15, 17*

Each time my thoughts are running wild, each time I am fearing the future, I can be assured that my times, however they come, are in God's hand. He is God, who can, does, and will help me!

So, how long does it take to heal? God only knows the answer, for He alone truly knows me and my needs. The work is already begun and God will never leave an unfinished project. I know He will not let me be ashamed.

My time of healing is in God's hand.

IS IT WORTH IT?

How can anything be worth the loss of a dear one for the rest of this life? How can it be worth this time of pain and the struggle of healing?

I am glad for God's patient work of comfort and growth in me. Now I am seeing that He is using me to show others His power.

Someone was challenged through the funeral service. It is worth it to share my eternal hope in Christ!

An unsaved friend is thinking and questioning. It is worth it to show the lost what God's salvation means in everyday life!

Little children, whom I have taught, have responded with assurance that my dear one is in heaven now. Once they barely knew what a Bible is. Now they are experiencing its truth and security. It is worth it to see them become settled in their faith!

A bereaved friend says that my letter to her brought joy and comfort. It is worth it to be able to understand another's hurt!

Committing my fears to my Lord, I went to a nursing home where I used to visit regularly. The folk said they knew my faith would sustain me and I would come back. God's honor was at stake! I had told them God lives in us and is sufficient in EVERY situation. It is worth it to be living proof of God's grace!

God wants us to confirm that we are His servants. We do this in patience, in distresses, by longsuffering, by the power of God, as sorrowful yet always rejoicing (*see* 2 Corinthians 6:1–10).

We will not be receiving His grace in vain. We will be bringing glory—honor resulting from a good opinion—to the One who gave His dearest and best for us.

That's worth it!

THIS END IS THE VERY BEGINNING

This is the end of our walking together for now. I must go where God leads me and you will want to do the same.

It is my sincere prayer that God has helped you lay hold on Him as we have shared the paths of our sorrow. That is how God planned it. He comforted me, so I could understand and share His comfort with you.

> Blessed be God. . .the Father of mercies,
> and the God of all comfort;
> who comforteth us in all our tribulation,
> that we may be able to comfort them
> which are in any trouble,
> by the comfort wherewith we ourselves
> are comforted of God.
> *2 Corinthians 1:3, 4*

All true comfort has its source in God.

This then is a beginning for you. Your life lies before you. Your God walks within you. He girds you with strength and will make your way perfect.

You've been dangling your feet in the pool of life, just dipping in a bit here and there to see how it goes. As He urges you to take the plunge, to get into the laps He's laid out for you, go right ahead! The waters may be somewhat of a shock at first. But they will be a soothing, healing balm as the days go by.

Have total confidence in your Heavenly Father's perfect choice for you.

Today is the very beginning of the rest of your life!

MY FUTURE—GOD'S PLAN

My future, Lord, what will it be?
    I wonder more and more.
The way You lead is beautiful;
    You're opening new doors.

Your plan conceived before time began
    Included all my days;
Thus I with wondering eyes and heart
    Must marvel at Your ways.

I scarce control my eagerness,
    As step by step you lead;
I glory in your personal care,
    Your every whisper heed.

And day by day and hour by hour,
    I'm astonished that it's I
For whom the God of everything
    Has such a watchful eye!

GOD'S FAITHFULNESS

A number of years have passed for me now. I want to testify to you that God has been unceasingly faithful. Oh, what a wonderful, loving, caring Father He is!

Each year has been a little easier than the previous one, though special dates on the calendar continued to be difficult for many years. Some people—those who hadn't experienced such a separation—didn't understand this, thought it silly. We must be considerate of their feelings, be glad that they have not had a broken heart.

Our memories will always be precious to us.

Yes, old places and faces continue to hold nostalgia and sometimes there are the familiar pangs of heartsickness. But these are less and less as time goes by.

That doesn't mean that I love my dear one less. I'm grateful that love is forever—not only for the duration of this life. But it does mean that I have left my dear one in God's safekeeping. We are instructed in Proverbs 4:25, 26 to let our eyes look straight ahead. God also promises that all our ways will then be ordered aright.

He has enabled me to go on and live the life He has chosen for me. By faith step out and walk with God. He will do the same for you.

LOOK RIGHT ON

Lift thine eyes, look on, my child,
    Look beyond the life that's nigh,
Look past sorrow, pain, and dying,
    Look beyond the azure sky.

Look beyond the world's horizon,
    Look beyond its hasty throng,
Look beyond its tarnished treasures,
    Yea, past time's relentless gong.

Look right on into the glory,
    Gaze a while on Jesus' face;
Contemplate how, made immortal,
    Thou in heaven shalt find thy place.

Then let thine eyes look straight before thee,
    Seeking naught but God's delight;
Press with all that is within thee,
    'Til thy faith's reward is sight!

IT'S A PERSONAL THING

Excuse me, please. I can't leave without asking one most important question.

Do you have a personal relationship with eternal God?

You may have read every word of this book and yet never experienced the peace and strength and hope that I have tried to share with you. These are mine because there was a time in my life when I accepted Jesus Christ as my personal Savior.

The way is simple:

ADMIT THAT YOU ARE A SINNER.

For all have sinned,
and come short
of the glory of God.
Romans 3:23

BELIEVE THAT JESUS IS GOD THE SON
AND HE PAID THE WAGES OF YOUR SIN.

For the wages of sin is death [eternal separation from God];
but the gift of God is eternal life through Jesus Christ our Lord.
Romans 6:23

CALL UPON GOD.

If thou shalt confess with thy mouth the Lord Jesus,
and shalt believe in thine heart that
God hath raised him from the dead,
thou shalt be saved.
Romans 10:9

Salvation is a very personal thing. It is between you and God. I cannot trust for you; no one can. The decision is yours alone.

I am praying for you.